# CONFUSION

### DARK POETRY BY
### R.E. TAYLOR

## SHADOWLIGHT PUBLISHING
## MACGREGOR, QUEENSLAND, AUSTRALIA 4109
### www.shadowlightbooks.com

# DEDICATION

I WOULD LIKE TO THANK MY FRIENDS, THE POETS AND ARTISTS OF THE WORLD, FOR THE INSPIRATION TO WRITE THE POETRY I HAVE PLACED WITHIN THESE PAGES AS WELL AS L.W. WHO KEPT ME FROM GOING OVER THE EDGE OF THE ABYSS.
I would also like to thank Liz Waterhouse for taking time to edit this work and make me a better poet!

# A World Named Delusion

A man's mind
Creative and intelligent
Mathematics, science and the arts came easy
He always strove to learn new things
There was nothing he wouldn't try
The world was his challenge and he did his best to defeat it
Questioning everything he made others think
However, years past and age took its toll
Grey hair came replacing the chestnut brown he had in his youth
Wrinkles surrounded tired eyes
Bones creaked and the body ached where it never hurt before
The mind that was once sharp as a knife dulled
Friends and family became unknown strangers
He struggled to recognize the people who loved him to no avail
The man's history becomes the present in his eyes
The dead come to life while the living do not exist
Doctors, nurses and family try to help
The man lives alone in his own world
This is the hell in an Alzheimer's world
Reality that is not real
Unknown sons, daughters, wives and husbands
A man alone without his memories
Without his life
A man all alone in a world he created
A world named delusion

# Lacking Control Of A Late Night Creative Mind

Sitting here for hours
Ideas flow through my mind
Some rush
Like water cascading toward the brink
Loud and roaring
Screaming to be heard
But moving too fast to be truly heard
Some crawl
Trying not to be noticed
Hiding behind the faster, louder ones
One thought stays in my mind
Fighting against the currents
Wanting to be written
Controlling my dreams
Demanding to be heard
Eyes fighting to sleep
Tired from a day of everything and nothing
A mind fighting to be creative
It wants me to write
I write what my heart tells me
My eyes cannot see the words
Thoughts flood my mind with new ideas
I finish as the sun rises
Another night with no sleep
Another morning with a new poem
Written by a poet
Words that mean everything and nothing
Except in a late night creative mind

# Perfection Lost

How in the world could I know?
What you are thinking?
What you are feeling?
I cannot tell from your words
There is love and warmth in your eyes
Your kisses are those of an angel
What thoughts are crossing your mind?
Are there doubts that you fear to express?
I know that you are my gift from the immortal gods
Thousands of prayers answered at once
One stroke of their hands created perfection
And perfection walked into my life
But there is a fear
Hiding in the darkness of my mind
What if tomorrow the gods rethink their gift?
They take you back and make you their own
I would never see you again
I would never know what you were thinking
What you were feeling
And I would be alone with my thoughts
My memories of perfection lost.

# One Pill or a Dozen

The world I see is tainted by life
Drugs cause me to be paranoid
Natural herbs the government made illegal
Pills to improve my mood
Others that bring me crashing down to Earth
A reality of flashing colored lights
Swirling around my mind
They block the real world from my reality
How many will make me feel pleasure?
One pill may be too few
A dozen, maybe too many
Chemicals mixing in my blood
Rushing into my paralyzed brain
Is the music I see real?
Are the colors I hear coming from nowhere?
Pink baby alligators dancing in the street
Doctor Who wearing a paisley skirt walks toward me
The Tardis has brightly colored polka dots of yellow and purple
They dance to the rhythm of the falling stars
Then the world fades away
Buildings and people turn into clouds
They blow away into a black velvet hurricane
I lie on the bed with my eyes clenched
Sweating and crying as my reality disappears
I call to The Doctor, but he isn't real
I crash back to Earth in a bloody heap
My eyes open and I see my bedroom
I will wait here for an eternity

At least it will feel like an eternity
Until I get another pill
Or maybe a dozen
And I leave again
Into my own reality
The reality where I am happy
At least until I die

# No More Me

I have asked for help
Been turned down
Been ignored
No one asked what was wrong
They all said things will get better
I waited
I hoped
I even prayed
But things got worse
My prayers fell on deaf ears
Hope died on the side of a lonely path
Yet I waited
Day after day
I saw people smiling
Laughing
Living life
Now I sit all alone
Not asking anyone for anything
A piece of steel in my hand
So thin, so sharp
One fast move
I watched as it moved as if in slow motion
There was no pain
A few moments of coldness
A minute of darkness
And suddenly things didn't matter
There was no more pain
No more tears
No more me

# That Beautiful Pain

That beautiful pain
The one that lives in my heart
Born the minute you leave
It takes away my sleep
Ripping my dreams apart
That beautiful pain
The one that only I know
I can never share it
Not that I would if I could
No one would ever understand
They do not see you as I do
That beautiful pain
The one that only fades when you return
Would I live without it?
Could I live without it?
Not if it meant that I would never have met you
That beautiful pain
I would rather suffer
Dealing with the hurt
Rather than lose you
And give the pain to another.

# Down The Sight Of A Rifle

Looking down the sights of his rifle
He sees people he was told were his enemies
Men, women and children walking down the street
Who are real enemies?
Who are innocents living their lives?
His finger tightens on the trigger
How could he know if his shot was true?
He watches the people carefully
Hearing his orders echo through his head
The order was given a half a world away
By men sitting in a room trying to raise the body count
They don't know the people their orders effect
They can't look into a new mother's eyes as she holds her baby
The trigger starts to tighten as the man obeys
The gun blasts forth a breath of flame
The bullet leaves not knowing its target
The bullet lands miles away never tasting blood
That day a soldier decided that no one would die
No one would be in the hospital because of him
That day he would be the hero who no one knows
He knew in his heart that he cared about other people
If only more thought like him
Felt like him
War would no longer exist
No humans would die needlessly
And there would be peace

# Trapped By An Inactive Mind

Your mind is hidden in darkness
Thoughts trapped in deep crevasses
Their screams echoes through deathly shadows
Attacked and strangled at their every move
The struggle against invisible shackles
Drawing blood as they fight their captor
Demons search for ideas ripping them apart
Stripped skin strewn across an evil world
A world created from depression and mania
Leaving the ideas disemboweled in the frenzied heat
Blood, skin and guts boil under the demon's breath
Screams of torture and pain fill the void left by random thoughts
Still alive, they choke on the stale sulfuric air
Waiting to die while hoping to be saved
A quick mind lights the darkness
Giving new life to near dead ideas
The strongest fight while the weakest wither and die
They rise through the darkness
Rising into the light they look back
They see the lost ideas dying beneath them
They care about what was lost
What ideas will never see the light of day
And they grieve as they come to light
And they will be told and retold
For that is what ideas are meant to be
Shared by the entire world not killed
Murdered by an inactive mind

# Scream Of the Bansee

I know the time has come
My heart is ready for its last beat
I can hear the Banshee calling
Its voice cuts through the demon in my head
A black carriage with gold trim
Darkly beautiful in the night
It watches as my heart beats its last
One raise of the scythe
A crook of a finger made of bone
But not a single word
Yet it smiled as I stepped in
My lifeless body laying behind me
It takes me to my final rest
A place or torment more that any I created
Still I am happy to be sitting on the black leather seat
Looking down upon the living world
I thank the Banshee for the scream I heard
And for the ride down the River Styx
For now I am home

# Incubus

I was born beneath a midnight sky
The moon traveled off its orbit
Casting ghostly images across my newly opened eyes
My soul was a sharpened sword
Created in the fires of Hell
Born into a world of pain and torture
The screams of the condemned were my lullaby
A thousand years of rage trapped in one heart
I watched you eat your own
Devouring the weaker souls
Sending the stronger to war fighting for bastards and freaks
You are the beast who calls me by name
Still shunning me as an upcoming evil
My mind was sharpened by ideas no one wanted
From my birth I began to fear the light
Worshipping the darkness of night
Demons and dark fae were my friends
Drinking and partying in underground clubs
People's nightmares were my fairy tale
My life began nursing on the blood of a succubus
Feeding on the flesh of the long dead
The bravest turn from me
Hiding in terror as I walk by
But I was born on the day that you were born
An unholy incubus created by man

Born to learn what you didn't want to know
To keep the knowledge away from your young

Yet, I knock on your door to tell you what I have learned
How to stop the carnage that I created for my father
You do not listen…you never listen
Just know that you have been warned
More and more die and murder
Incurable illnesses ravage the lands
All done in my name
Now, I lay you down to sleep
You better cross your heart before you die
I will be waiting when you awake
And you will know the hell that awaits you
Your soul will be mine so that I may punish you
Torture you for what you have done

# Do Not Fear The Weeping Angel

Do not fear the weeping angel
She has watched for centuries
Unable to help, she merely wacthes
Hands covering her face as she cries
Her tears flow for the bodies piled beneath her
Men killed in a senseless war
The souls wandering in torment
The children left behind
She cries for the babies, left at her feet
Newborn and innocent
The reach for their mothers
Crying for milk, fighting for life
Their mothers do not know
Or do not care about the love they left behind
She weeps for the homeless man, beaten and starving
Begging for change or a small piece of food
Freezing without a coat or blanket
Dying on cold stone... Alone
Her eyes of stone, her hidden face
Shows more love to lost souls than any living being
Her tears are not those of a statue
They were not given to her by those who created her
They come from God
A message, a sign for anyone to care

# The Girl In The Window

How could anyone ever forget?
Such beautiful paintings
Each hung carefully
Lit with just the right light
People walk by day after day
They look but they are not looking
They see such a memorable picture
A city at its glory,
Berlin in the beginning of the Third Reich
A thousand red flags with black broken crosses
People wearing colorful clothes
Each with a smile on their faces
A paradise on planet Earth
They look but they are not looking
They do not see right in front of them
Hiding in a window is a young girl
A girl of no more than nine years old
Such pain and torture can be seen as she reaches for help
There is a tiny six pointed yellow star on her chest
Even sixty five years later no one sees her
No one sees the secret the artist put in his world
Could people be so blind to someone in need?
Did that little girl live?
Was she tortured and killed alone in a prison camp
Her story was never told
But she did more that even the toughest soldier
Her innocent face, the tears flowing down her cheeks
She cried for help for six million people
It was all there painted for us to see.
If only anyone had taken the time to look.

# Is There Really A Reality

Who says that we are who we are?
Are we really someone else's reality?
Do we have our own identity?
Am I who I see in the mirror?
Do I really see what is before me?
Or am I only what my mind wants me to see?
How can I know what is real?
What I should accept as true?
Is there really something called real?
Or is reality actually nothing?
Could it all be a fantastic dream?
Do I have to trust others to tell me?
Do they know the truth?
What do they see when they look at me?
Are they even real?
Am I real for that matter?
Does it matter in the grand scheme?
Am I everything?
Am I nothing?
I know, at least in my mind, I am real
Maybe?

# No One Ever Asks Why

I look around at the people today
Wondering what happened to happier times
People die from making love
No one ever asks why
Children are shot while they play
No one ever asks why
Our heroes show people how to cheat and lie
No one ever asks why
Teens spend their lives before a lit screen
climbing towers and shooting innocent people
Death has become a game
No one ever asks why
Others have forgotten how to talk
Guns, bullets and knives speak for them
No one ever asks why
Kids learn to hate before they can talk
They listen to their parent's hate
and grow up not questioning.
No one ever asks why
People kill in the name of their God
although they all believe in the same god
No one ever asks why
Young men die on a field miles away
not knowing, and not asking, why
No one ever asks why
Our friends become our enemies
Our enemies become our friends
No one ever asks why.
Why doesn't someone ask?

# Mommie

Mommie, I was born just hours ago
You looked at me
My eyes were barely open and I could see your face
You were happy for a moment
Then your look changed to hatred
What could I have done in such a short time?
Was I that bad of a child that you despised me?
I know I cried
Calling for your love for just a moment
But you would not let me look into your eyes
Now, I lay in the cold winter's winds
There are no blankets to keep me warm
Rotting food surrounds me
I am too young to survive on it
I cry harder than I ever had before
Yet, no one hears me or no one cares
Half of my life I have been alone
Something no baby should ever feel
Tonight, will be my first night
Tonight, will be my last night
I never even had the chance to be held
Never had the chance to smile
Never had to chance to be loved
I just have the chance to die

# The Reality Hiding Inside Of A Needle

One little shot, A mere pinch in a throbbing vein
Liquid injected by a shaking hand
The reality of life falls away
The sky turns a deep crimson
As birds fly toward a leafless tree
Branches covered with newly born dragons
Breathing fire and inhaling toxic smoke
The watch their surroundings
Looking for a single flower
Where butterflies mate in unending rhythm
Giving birth to newly hatched rainbows
Red, violet, blue, green and yellow
All fading into blacks and grays
As they rise to take their place in the sky
White fluffy clouds wrap around the arches
,Like tendrils of a parasitic vine
Strangling the life from the lifeless prisms
Dissolving their shades into an invisible spectrum
Their darkness falls eclipsing the nearest star
Open eyes strain in the dimming light
They are looking for a floating eagle
Golden wings rising on heated air
It flies around the sky
Leaving a trail of blue skies and morning light
It is the one creature who knows reality
What true reality should be like
At least until the next little shot
The pinch in another throbbing vein
Takes it all away again

# The Old Man In The Mirror

Who is that old man who looks at me in the morning?
When I shave and shower, he is there,
 living in a pane of glass
Grey hairs replacing the dark walnut brown
More and more each day, each hour
Eyes looking tired from ages of struggles
Each reflecting a soul which was once so full of life
Now it lays stagnant and lost
It has the memories of its youth
Doing this that that man can only now remember
Wrinkles took so long to show
Even fooling that old man into thinking he was younger than he
is
Every grey hair, every wrinkle has been earned
They are the wages of pain and anxiety of aging
Some called them badges of honor
I look in the mirror and see that man looking back at me
I don't see honor, pain, stress or anxiety
That old man looking back at me has lived a full life
Successes and mistakes of the past are reflected in the mirror
Lost loves and loves found are hidden in his spirit
I look at the old man in the mirror
I look at the grey hair and the sad eyes
I see each and every wrinkle
I look at the old man in the mirror and I see life

# Nice Party

I see my best friend
He is face down in a gutter filled with vodka, gin and tequila
We watched as he drank one after another after another
Someone tried to stop him before he did anything stupid
We told him he was going to get hurt
But the more he drank the bigger he got
The bigger he got, the more attitude he had
The more attitude he had, the more he drank
Finally, it came down to a girl
A young one, no more than 16 with a fake id and a leather skirt
around her not so virgin hips.
We saw it, but he was blind to everything but her
Her top showed more than anyone could expect
Barely able to walk, he stepped over to her
And told her how beautiful she was
She kissed him as her father walked in
It was a deep, passionate kiss we all desire
Her father broke a beer glass and a chair
The pool cue was next and finally the window
That welcomed everyone to the dancing and music
I walked out
My best friend was in the gutter filled with vodka, gin and
tequila
He looked at me said two words and passed out
I will always remember what he said, "Nice party."
Just before the police came and took him away.

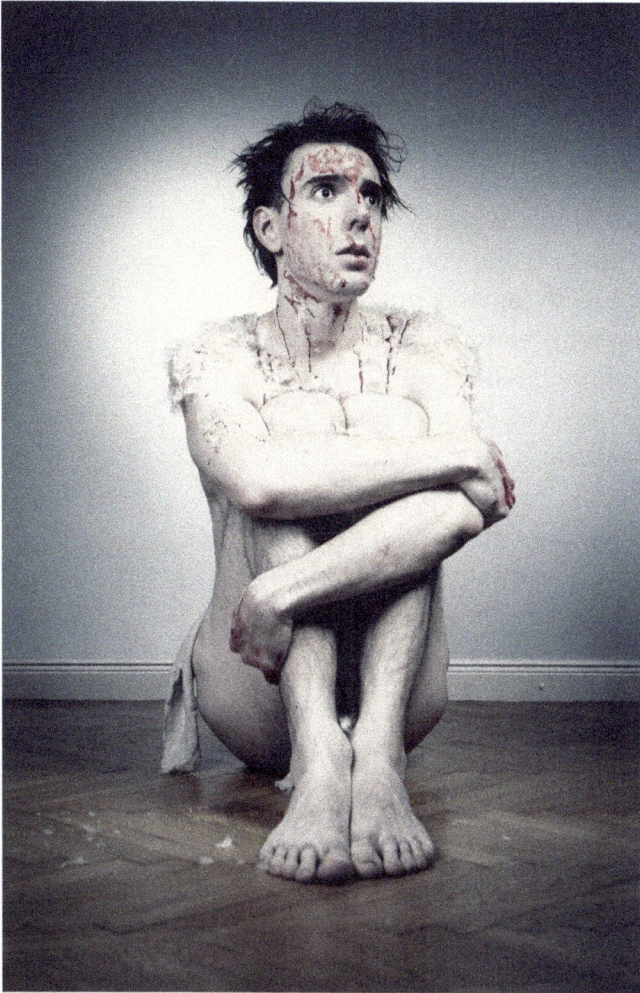

# The End Of An Argument

You lie next to me
Your body glistening in the yellow moonlight
Damp with sweat from the August air
How much I long to kiss you
I want so badly to tell you I love you
You back presses against my chest
I can feel your breathing, your heartbeat
But you will not make a sound
My empty arms try to hold you
But you pull away
Retreating into your deep silent world
Is there anything you want to say?
Or did you say it all during our fight?
A silly fight we never should have had
Now I long for your voice
To look into your eyes
I pray for our feet to touch
So that I can know that we will be alright
And I can love you again

# Sitting Alone At The Midnight Bar At 2:00 a.m.

You were there every night
Sitting alone
Nursing a watered down Jack Daniels
Cigarettes burned out on the table
Another lit, but dying in your lips
You spent time hiding in the darkness
Shielded by the light
Your eyes glowed with an icy hue
Red claws dug into the table
Gouging deep into the wood
You teeth dug deep into your tender lips
Maybe you never knew
Everyone talked about you
Never a loud word
Just whispers kept away from you
Maybe by fear
A fear that you would attack
Tearing the person's heart out
Holding it in your hands as it beat its last
You wonder why no one spoke to you
Not even a passing hello
What would you have said?
Would you have let the darkness open
Even the slightest crack
Or would you have pulled it tight
Wrapping your body in its safeety
Would it be worth the risk?
No one will ever know
For the rest of your life
You will be there every night

Sitting alone

Nursing a watered down Jack Daniels
Cigarettes burned out on the table
Another lit, but dying in your lips
Spending time hiding in the darkness
Shielded by the light
All alone
The angel of nightmares
The demons of dreams

# There's Always Time For A Swim

Standing by the lake
So calm and blue
A cool breeze blowing in from Canada
Blue skies above
The sun making glistening diamonds in the waves
It seems so tranquil, almost inviting me to walk in
I look again, behind me all is stress and turmoil
Hiding in the trees, weeds and flowers
Below the waves lies eternal rest
The quiet that only Poseidon can provide
I watch the waves lapping onto the shore
Their fantasies draw me closer
Begging me to join them
To be with them
How far could I get
When would the waves envelop me?
Taking me into their darkness
There is no way to know even if they would
I look for a distant shore
But it is not there
I wonder what it would be like
Then I turn away
Looking again at the peaceful water
I walk down the beach
Looking at the blue sky, the white sun
And I see a glimmer of hope
I decide that the waves can wait
The dreaminess of Poseidon's rest
Can wait for another day
There is always time for a swim

# The Animal In The Cage

Locked in a cage
Steel bars of my own making
The floor lined with the bodies of those who came before
Alongside the bones of those who conspired to harm me
My fingers claw in desperation
Ripping the flesh from the ends
Exposing claws lost eons ago through evolution
My teeth tear into the metal, filling
 my mouth with orange powder
Powder that corrodes my throat making it impossible to talk
Impossible to scream or plead for my life
Alas, the more I try to escape the smaller the cage becomes
Compressing my hopes and dreams
Shrinking any spirit or soul I may have left.
Why would the owner of the cage treat me so?
Men, women and children walk by my cage
Pointing and laughing at the animal trying to escape
They must know the pain I am in
Maybe they can see past the hatred I feel
Maybe they can see the torture  in my eyes
All they have to do is look
Maybe if just one person looked and saw the real me
One bar would fade and I would be released
Maybe I could be human again
If only just one person took the time
The time to see that the animal before them was a man
If just…

# I Am Human

My eyes shut for another night
Images flow across my eyes
Some grey clouds on the horizon
Birds fly by going nowhere
A stagnant lake lies before me
Not a single wave or ripple
The birds swoop and die before me
Dragons and demons tear the world apart
Leaving me in a world of complete dark
Screams of pain and terror
They fill the early moments of sleep
Somewhere pleasure comes from the suffering
I want to open my eyes
The terror holds them shut
Not allowing me a chance to escape
I can feel them tearing into my mind
I don't care what they do to me
This world is one of my design
Scary and deadly to others
It is my home
It is where I choose to be
Alone and fighting an unseen enemy
Yet, knowing that I am immortal
I am a god in my world
The all powerful god of the underworld
I will reign until the sun rises so far away
And I change into a mortal human
With all their faults and foibles
I am human

# Mister Nobody

He sits quietly
Not eating for days
Hoping for strangers to toss him a coin
He begged for money
A sandwich
Or even for someone to just smile
Hundreds of people passed him
Three piece suits
Designer dresses
Twenty dollar cigars
They looked, but they could not see
Maybe they choose not to see
They never talked to the man
They never knew he was a hero in WW II
He was a prisoner in Korea
He retired while in Vietnam
Never asking about his wife and kids
Killed by a man
Drunk while driving
They never stood a chance
At that moment he lost his reason for living
At that moment he lost his mind
Gone were the children's laughter
Gone was the love of his life
Gone was the home where he loved them
Gone was the man
Spending time hiding in basements
Sleeping in cardboard boxes
He survived
But he never lived again

Nobody saw him that cold December night
Snow covered the ground
Ice covered his hair and beard
He simply ceased to be
Now they look at the place where he always sat
Something is missing but no one knows what
He will not be missed
He will not be mourned
He will be lost except in the memory of one person
Who took the time
To talk
To listen
To remember

# Life In Death Valley

I stand alone
The heat of the day burns my skin
The cold of the night chills to the bone
There is no shelter
No hope in sight
The sand whips around tearing my skin
Mountainous dunes come and go in minutes
A trillion bits of ancient rocks
Lifted and ground forever, they drift in the winds
Settling in sculptures created by Hades
Pictures of beauty
Signs of a coming death
Nothing lasts in this alien world
Skulls and bones of those who passed before
Bleached white by an unrelenting sun
They rest alone…the last vestiges of a lost life
One hundred miles of hell with no water
Nothing for life to continue

# An American soldier

A 20 year old veteran sits on the sidewalk
His legs blown off in the Iraqi sand
He obeyed Washington when they told him to fight
He killed when he was told to
He served his country the best he could
Now he has no job and no home
Most people walk by him without a glance
He collects pennies just to buy a hamburger
Money given him by people driving fancy cars
He spends his nights in a shelter
Sharing a room with drug addicts and lunatics
The government doesn't care about him
He lost that when he lost his legs
He will continue to fight
He will fight for food or a bed
He will fight to keep his dignity
What little dignity he has left
He will live and he will be remembered by someone
Maybe by the person who gave him 25 cents one morning
Then again, maybe no one will remember him
After all, he was just a beggar on the street
And who remembers them

# Death On A Darkened Street

A darkened street
The amber glow of an old lamp
Doing little to chase the shadows
A young boy lies bleeding
Beaten, battered and barefoot
Wounds puncture his heart and lungs
Barely thirteen he grasps at bloody clothes
And he cries
He never had the chance to live or love
Alone on the street, he calls for his mother
His eyes close
A sigh comes from his lips
And he is gone
Killed for a pair of shoes

# The Frozen Pathway To Your Heart

I never could find the way
It is a path few have traveled
If you ever allowed anyone
The path is treacherous
Full of pitfalls and deep valley
I don't think anyone made it all the way
You'd ever leave an opening
Not even the slightest crack
Cold winds blow out from the valley
Covering the path with ice and frost
Hiding the footprints
Covering the bodies of those who came before
The few who made it this far
Not knowing the right words
The right actions
They gave up hope
Not knowing that over the next hill
Lies a door with a golden lock
Waiting for a young knight
To have the right words
With the right feeling
Only then the paths will thaw
The winds will warm
The walls will crack
The lock to you heart will open
You'll let someone love you
And maybe once again
You will be able to love again

# History Lost To A New Generation

Where is our history?
Grandparents tell their tall tales
Walking twenty miles to school
Barefoot
Uphill
Knee deep in snow
The children laugh but they don't listen
Grandparents also tell stories of the old days
Living history wanting to be learned
Waiting in line for a five cent apple
Rooms lit by a single gas flame
Meat and sugar rationed
Barely enough to live
Men hauled off to war, a half a world away
The children don't listen
Days of mourning over a lost president
Nuclear missiles off the Florida shore
Cars without FM radios
Black and white television
Sport greats without drugs
Dr Pepper with a peanut
Schools without gunshots fired in anger
The children don't listen
Four students killed for speaking their minds
A war we could never have won
Long hair and bell-bottoms
People looking for a peace
The children don't listen
Grandparents die
Taking their stories with them

Locking their history in silent lips
Unable to share the lives
History lost forever
Maybe the children should have listened

# The Power Of God

Neon flames burn into midnight's blackness
Lighting the forest's dense foliage
Yellowish orange light dances
Across the emerald green leaves
Casting ebony shadows into the night
Violet smoke, with tints of grey
Creating a web carried aloft by every breeze
A deathly silence fills the woods
As the Moon casts its silver light down from the sky
It is hauntingly eerie
As if it was a world alien to all without an imagination
What do the animals see when they look from their dens?
Do they look or do they hide their eyes under the ground?
Does the Man in the Moon see the world he protects?
What does he think of what it has become?
Shadows and light, smoke and flame and a gentle breeze
Is this the world that God created?
Or is this the world of darkness and demons?
Created by the most evil of evils
The stars above know the truth as they wait in Heaven
They know that the morning's light will let the universe know
The beauty hidden by the darkness
Was there all of the time
Waiting
Waiting until God turned the Earth
And His light returns to give love
Giving hope to those who wait out the darkness
To those who believe in Him and his power

# Dreams Floating In An Eternal Darkness

Blackness surrounding me
Streaked with differing shades of grey
Shards of hope fly by
Shattered dreams from ages past
Reflecting the total lack of light
Just out of my grasp
Why are they here teasing me?
Making me think that there is a chance
That there may be a way out
I look
Scanning the darkness
I watch the shimmering hope float by
At the tips of my extended fingers
Then I realize that it is a vain effort
Hope will never come to me
I resign myself to the eternal blackness
To grasp for dreams
That I will never ever reach

I Died Today

I died today
I know that you will not shed a tear
You know my life was yours
I was sad when you left
I was so happy when you came hope
Still, I was scared at the same time
I didn't behave the way you wanted me to
I did do bad things
I ate your shoes
I peed on the floor
You never taught me what you wanted
All I wanted to do was please you
My life was made whenever we went for a walk
You never had the time
So I sat by the door while you watched the TV
All I wanted was to be your friend
But you didn't care
I know you loved me once
You played we me
We walked for miles
And I got all the petting you could give me
But, that doesn't matter
I died today
Killed by a stranger in a white room
I do know that you will not cry
You will not even remember that I died today

# An overprotected Heart

A broken heart
Pieces kept together by razor wire
Such pain
Wounds from the last moment I saw you
Did you know that your words had such power?
Did you know that my heart would fall apart?
No silk threads would seal the chasms
It frayed and tore with every word
Not a drop of blood was spilt
There was none left after your attack
The sharpness of the razor wire
Its shiny points wrapped around my heart
Stabbing into the gentle muscle
Drops of blood on the tip of every blade
They remind me of your words
The hurt you caused
It stops others from getting in
Not giving them the chance to do what you did
My heart is protected from hurt
From you and your meanness
Protected from love and happiness
All because of you

# Instant Fires of Lost Hope

Distant fires
Smoke rises into a cloudless sky
Cries of torment fill the blackened sky
Stars sparkle as they look down
They see a world depressed
No money
No food
No hope
The peop;e raise their eyes
Looking to the heavens
Trying to find a spark
A sign that everything will be alright
Planets traverse the blackness
A million stars shine brightly
Too far away to hear a prayer
All the voices crying in the night
Calling for a being who will care
Asking for a little piece of hope
The stars, the planets, hear,,
 but continue on their travels
They do not listen
They do not care
We are on our own
We are all alone

# More Children Die

Children dying
Not given a chance to live
To Learn
To Love
Taken by another
Trying to show the world
Making a name against those who they hate
Innocents who merely are there
In a good place
At a very bad time
Dances, classes, alone in their rooms
Peace is broken by madness
Sharp sounds
Deep pain
Never ending darkness
Back in the light
Parents cry
Memories flow
Friends mourn
Somewhere, someone sees the story
A newscaster tells of death
They don't cry
They don't mourn
They plan
They dream of darkness
They dream of death

They look for a good place at a bad time
They look into innocent eyes
And they kill
The cycle starts again
And more children die

# The Curse Of The H.M.S. Dutchman

An ancient ship
Black sails raised
They reach for any breeze
Ignored by Calypso
Feared by men and spirits alike
Lost souls wander the unpolished deck
Waiting in unbearable heat
As souls drift by on tattered boats
Screaming for release
Knowing they are bound for eternity
Some scramble aboard
Prisoners of time
Part of a decaying ship
Never able to leave
Watching the land pass by
Cool waterfalls
Lush green forests
Cool breezes blow from the white sands
Taunting their burning eyes
Allowing only a moment hope
Before entering the endless hopelessness
The last glimpse of sunset
Says goodbye to the condemned
Before they start an eternity of nothing
A never ending punishment
That not even death can end

# The Story Of The Missing Word

One word
A gathering of letters and sounds
Keeping me from saying what I want to say
I knew the word
It came to me in a dream
Along with a hundred others
Traveling through my unconscious
Another reality
Not connected to my own
I should have written it down
Kept it next to my bed
It was perfect
Just the right tone and rhythm
Why didn't I open my eyes?
The pen was next to the bed
I've used it a hundred times before
I couldn't, wouldn't interrupt that word
I knew it wasn't mine to own
But, I wanted to watch it
See where it wanted to go
What it wanted to say
I never wanted it to leave
I wanted to hold it forever
But, it flew away
Into the stars with a million other words

Thousands of unfinished poems
A billion lost thoughts
Until it comes back
If it ever comes back
The poem will sit unfinished
The story will never be...

# The Endless Tick Tock Of The Clock

The endless tick tock
Echoing off the walls and into my mind
A clock hangs on the wall
Counting the seconds
The minutes
The hours
The time that makes up my life
Does it know anything about me?
Can it see the stress it causes me?
Every tick shortens my life
Every tock brings me closer to my end
My mind wanders
It wonders
Have I led a happy life?
Have I made others happy?
One day my heart knows
My mind remembers
The clock will stop
My life will fade and I will never know
Have I had any effect on anyone?
Have I made one person smile?
Did I matter?

# Please Lord: A Soldier's Prayer

Dear Lord,
Please tell my son that I was sorry
that I was not there when he was born
Tell him that missed his first step and
The first time he said "Dada"
Tell him that his first day of school was a
story his mommy told me in a letter from home
Let him know that I wish I could be there to play
catch with him on a hot summer day,
and I will not be the one to cheer him,
when he pitches his first no-hitter.
I will not see the light in his eye when he brings home his
first of many true loves and I will not be there when he
finally chooses the one
I will not be there to hear his son scream
at the first moment of life and "papa" will not be there to
hold him.
Dear Lord, please do not tell him,
that when You last saw me,
I was laying face down in Iraq
The sand stained with my blood
 But make sure to tell him that with my last breath
I said for you to tell him that I love him.

# Standing at the Gates of Heaven

Standing at the gates of Heaven
I look between the bars
Such a paradise just beyond
Kept out of my reach
I am only allowed to watch
Gargoyles block my way
Holding me back
They rip at my cloaks
Tearing them to shreds
Black angels sing my praises
Wrapping leather wings around me
Holding my breaths, deep in my chest
They tear at my heart
Pulling my arteries from my chest
Drawing my blood onto the floor
They laugh at my unending pain
Enjoying the torture they inflict
I am drawn away to a hell of my own making
Watching eternity from a molten rock
From now until the end of days
Snakes and demons will be my only friends
Existing only in my private hell

# I Am Not A Poet

I am not a poet
I have not suffered enough
Seen enough strife and pain
I haven't experienced the truth of life
I have lost the visions of hope
Replacing them with hatred and despair
I know that I have seen beauty
The images are locked away in lost memories
Yes, I have seen fields of flowers
All I can see is what is on their surfaces
The blues, reds and golds of each
But, I do not know their hidden meaning
What lies beneath each petal?
It is not that I may not see
I may just not care
After all a flower is just a flower
Something to be looked at and admired
Nothing more
Nothing less
So how can I be a poet?
When I cannot see what is underneath?

# A Crack In The Wall

I look both right and left
All I see is a wall made of stone and brick
There are no openings
There are no cracks
I know why it was built
How was it built?
Who laid the first brick
Did it start the day we met?
Did I say the wrong thing?
Was it that I didn't love you the way you wanted?
Am I the only one who created the wall?
I tried to reach you, but it was already too high
My heart would not lift me high enough to even see over
What is on your side?
Are you happy there?
Do you have any cracks?
Is there one single brick missing?
One brick where feelings can slip through
If that one brick is gone
If there is a single space
My love can find its way through
Then and only then will the wall crumble
Turning into piles of hate
Piles we can ignore
And we can love again

# The World Of A Drug Induced Coma

Do you see me?
Do you even hear a single word I say?
Is the universe you are in the same as mine?
Did you see the tears I shed as I looked at you?
Or did the chemicals change your reality?
I wish that you could tell me
Yours eyes are closed and unmoving
Twitching and shifting
Yet unable to open
Unable to see me watching you
I think that you may know that I am there
Yet, I wonder what you are dreaming about
What thoughts are running through your mind?
When you awake will you tell me?
Will you even remember what they were?
I will wait until you are ready
Watching you until you awaken
Until your eyes open and you smile again
When I hear you say hello
Only then will I know that everything is alright

# Memories Of An Old Depression Era Store

You sit there
Grey and beaten from the years
Your door hangs from but a single hinge
Windows busted from little boys just being boys
A faded Coca Cola sign hangs by one nail
Above a rusted metal roof
It wasn't always like that
How many children rushed through that door
Pennies in hand
Looking for a piece of candy
Maybe an ice cream on a hot day
Old people used to gather with you
Playing checkers
Drinking a cold pop
Or just talking about a woman down at the corner
You were always there for them
They needed you more than they knew
Now you sit
Alone and rotting
The children who rushed your door
Now they take their children to the mall
Impersonal and cold
The old people sit in nursing homes
They watch TV with blank eyes
And they wait
Wait for the next dose of their numbing medication

There are none  of the laughs we shared
There are none of the memories you gave
You were passed by (not what they now want}
Maybe old before your time
Some will remember and they will drive by
Looking at you
Remembering that one bottle of pop
Thinking back to the story the old man told about the war
They will remember you
Your open door and your checker board
And a happier time.

# Lacking control of A Late Night Creative Mind

Sitting here for hours
Ideas flow through my mind
Some rush
Like water cascading toward the brink
Loud and roaring
Screaming to be heard
But moving too fast to be truly heard
Some crawl
Barely moving
Trying not to be noticed
Hiding behind the faster, louder ones
One thought stays in my mind
Fighting against the currents
Wanting to be written
Controlling my dreams
Demanding to be heard
Eyes fighting to sleep
Tired from a day of everything and nothing
A mind fighting to be creative
It wants me to write
My soul surrenders
I write what my heart tells me
My eyes cannot see the words
Thoughts flood my mind with new ideas
I finish as the sun rises

Another night with no sleep
Another morning with a new poem
Written by a poet
Words that mean everything and nothing
Except in a late night creative mind

# There's Always Time For A Swim

Standing by the lake
So calm and blue
A cool breeze blowing in from Canada
Blue skies above
The sun making glistening diamonds in the waves
It seems so tranquil
Almost inviting me to walk in
I look again
Behind me there is stress and turmoil
Hiding in the trees, weeds and flowers
Below the waves lies eternal rest
The quiet that only Poseidon can provide
I watch the waves lapping onto the shore
Their fantasies draw me closer
Begging me to join them
To be with them
How far could I get
When would the waves envelop me?
Taking me into their darkness
There is no way to know even if they would
I look for a distant shore
But it is not there
I wonder what it would be like
Then I turn away
Looking again at the peaceful water


I walk down the beach
Looking at the blue sky, the white sun

And I see a glimmer of hope
I decide that the waves can wait
The dreaminess of Poseidon's rest
Can wait for another day
The is always time for a swim

# Glass Heart

Such a fragile organ
A heart made of glass
Born pure and flawless
Filled with undying love
It ages with cracks and flaws
Some visible to the naked eye
Some so small they cannot be seen
Every heart of glass breaks
Shatters deep within the soul
Shards can never be replaced
The broken heart can never be fixed
it simply dies a painful death
At least it can feel no pain

# Untitled

A million nights in the darkness
Just my thoughts to keep me company
Poems and songs that will never be written
Memories of loves lost decades
Apologizes that I should have made
Changes in my life that never should have happened
Rarely a dream struggles to get through
Dreams that quickly turn into vicious nightmares
Demons ripping into my soul
Despite a billion other souls struggling to survive
No one to hear my screams through the darkness
My past haunts my every moment
Although I am not ashamed of what I have done
I am afraid of what the past holds for me
What the future has to offer
Death and suffering
Pain beyond a mortal's endurance
Loneliness and grief
And maybe a fleeting, rare moment of happiness
Just enough for a second of hope
Then it will be gone

Check out R.e. Taylor's other books:

Available at www.shadowlightbooks.com

www.ingramcontent.com/pod-product-compliance
Lightning Source LLC
Chambersburg PA
CBHW070759050426
42452CB00012B/2405